D1462476

Daniel
and the
Tattletales

Daniel 6

(Daniel in the Lions' Den)

Mary Manz Simon
Illustrated by Dennis Jones

CPH

SAINT LOUIS

Dedicated to Christian retailers
Philippians 1:3–6

Books by Mary Manz Simon from Concordia Publishing House

Hear Me Read Level 1 Series
What Next?
Drip Drop
Jibber Jabber
Hide the Baby
Toot! Toot!
Bing!
Whoops!
Send a Baby
A Silent Night
Follow That Star
Row the Boat
Rumble, Rumble
Who Will Help?
Sit Down
Come to Jesus
Too Tall, Too Small
Hurry, Hurry!
Where Is Jesus?

Hear Me Read Big Book Series
Drip Drop
Who Will Help?
Sit Down
Where Is Jesus?

Hear Me Read Level 2 Series
The No-Go King
Hurray for the Lord's Army
The Hide-and-Seek Prince
Daniel and the Tattletales
The First Christmas
Through the Roof
A Walk on the Waves
Thank You, Jesus

Little Visits ® Series
Little Visits on the Go
Little Visits for Toddlers
Little Visits with Jesus
Little Visits Every Day

Stop! It's Christmas
God's Children Pray
My First Diary

Copyright © 1993 Concordia Publishing House
3558 S. Jefferson Avenue, St. Louis, MO 63118-3968
Manufactured in the United States of America

Library of Congress Cataloging-in-Publication Data

Simon, Mary Manz, 1948–
    Daniel and the tattletales : Daniel 6 : Daniel in the lions' den; Mary Manz Simon; illustrated by Dennis Jones.
       p.   cm. — (Hear me read. Level 2)
    Summary: A simple retelling of the Bible story in which Daniel is thrown into the lions' den.
    ISBN 0-570-04733-1
    1. Daniel (Biblical character)—Juvenile literature. 2. Bible stories. English—O.T. Daniel. [1. Daniel (Biblical character) 2. Bible stories—O.T.] I. Jones, Dennis, ill. II. Title. III. Title: Daniel and the lions' den. IV. Series: Simon, Mary Manz, 1948– Hear me read. Level 2.
BS580. D2S46 1993
224′.509505—dc20
                                            92-31887

6 7 8 9 10 11 12 13   07 06 05 04 03 02 01 00

"There goes Daniel," said Prince One.
"He is working again."

"He works all the time,"
said Prince Two.
"He does a good job too."

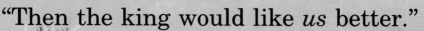

"I wish Daniel would get into trouble,"
said Prince Three.
"Then the king would like *us* better."

Prince One, Prince Two, and Prince
Three watched Daniel.
They watched Daniel work hard.
They listened when Daniel told
the truth.
They grumbled when the king smiled
at Daniel.

"Let's spy on Daniel," said Prince One.
"Maybe we can get him into trouble."

Prince One, Prince Two, and
Prince Three watched Daniel.
They watched Daniel work.
Daniel worked hard.

Prince One, Prince Two, and
Prince Three peeked in the window.
They watched Daniel.
Daniel knelt down and folded
his hands.
Daniel prayed to God.

Prince One, Prince Two, and
Prince Three listened at the palace.
Daniel talked to the king.
The king smiled at Daniel.

Prince One, Prince Two, and
Prince Three peeked in the window.
They watched Daniel.
Daniel knelt down and folded
his hands.
Daniel prayed to God.

Prince One, Prince Two, and
Prince Three grumbled.
"Daniel is too good," said Prince One.
"Daniel works and prays," said Prince Two.
"He works and prays, works and prays,"
said Prince Three.

"That's it!"
They all jumped up.
"That's it!"

"Daniel prays to God," said Prince One.
"Daniel prays to God every day."

"The king can make a new law," said Prince Two.
"Everybody must pray to the king!"

"People who don't pray to the king will be punished," said Prince Three.
"People who don't pray to the king will be thrown into the lions' den."

Prince One, Prince Two, and
Prince Three put on their finest clothes.
They wore their best smiles.
They walked to the palace.

"Your Majesty," said Prince One.

"Your Majesty, you are so wonderful," said Prince Two.

"Your Majesty, people should pray to you," said Prince Three.

The king listened to Prince One.
He listened to Prince Two.
He listened to Prince Three.
The king liked the idea.
He made a new law.

"Everybody must pray to me,"
commanded the king.
"No one may pray to God.
People who disobey will be thrown into
the lions' den."

Daniel heard about the new law.
Daniel went home to pray.

Prince One, Prince Two, and
Prince Three peeked in the window.

Daniel knelt down and folded his
hands.
He did not pray to the king.
Daniel prayed to God.

"Your Majesty," said Prince One, "your new law says everyone should pray to you."

"But someone is praying to God," said
Prince Two.
"Someone is disobeying you."

"That is not good," said the king.
"This person must be punished.
He must be thrown into the lions' den.
Who is this person?"

"Daniel," said Prince Three.
"Daniel prays to God."

The king was sad.
The king liked Daniel.
He did not want Daniel to be hurt.
But he could not help him.

The king commanded sadly, "Throw Daniel into the lions' den."

Prince One, Prince Two, and
Prince Three smiled.

The king went to bed.
He was so upset; he could not sleep.
The king was awake all night.

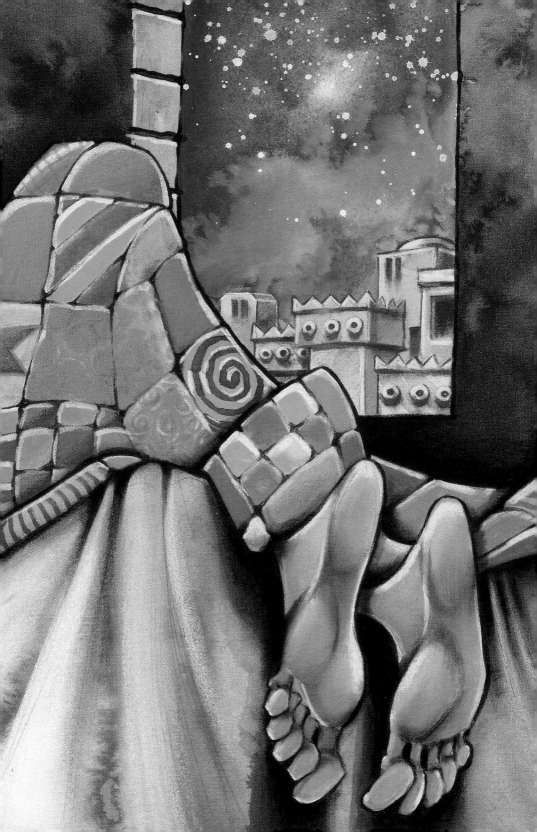

In the morning the king ran to the lions' den.
"Daniel," called the king.
"Daniel, did your God save you?"

"Yes, your majesty," Daniel called back.
"God sent an angel to keep me safe from
the lions.
God saved me."

The king commanded, "Take Daniel out of the lions' den.
Throw Prince One, Prince Two, and Prince Three into the lions' den."

Then the king commanded, "Everyone must pray to Daniel's God.
God protected Daniel from the lions.
Daniel's God is the real God!"

About the Author

Mary Manz Simon holds a doctoral degree in education with a specialty in early childhood education. She has taught at levels from preschool through postgraduate. Dr. Simon also has authored *Stop! It's Christmas; God's Children Pray;* the best-selling *Little Visits with Jesus; Little Visits Every Day; Little Visits for Toddlers; Little Visits on the Go; My First Diary,* and the Hear Me Read Level 1 Bible stories series. She and her husband, the Reverend Henry A. Simon, are the parents of three children.